Low Sodium Instant Pot Cookbook

An Essential Guide to Reducing Sodium and Fat in Your Diet (American Heart Association Slow Cooker Cookbook)

Laurel Pitre

Readers acknowledge that the author is not engaging in the rendering of legal, financial, medical or professional advice.

By reading this document, the reader agrees that under no circumstances are we responsible for any losses, direct or indirect, which are incurred as a result of the use of information contained within this document, including, but not limited to, errors, omissions, or inaccuracies.

Table of contents

Introduction

Diet is a critical and crucial aspect of any human's life. How you eat and what you eat ultimately determines how your body will stay in the long journey ahead.

While various edible factors may hamper the well-being of your heart and health, perhaps one of the more substantial one these days is "Sodium," "NaCl" or simply called "Table Salt."

With the rise of fast food joints, processed meats, canned goods, etc. the exposure to Sodium is at all time high these days!

And the effects are apparent.

Recent statistics have shown that almost 90%+ Americans consume too much sodium and nearly 75 million American adults suffer from hypertension, which rounds up to every 1 in 3 American adults!

Not only has that, but 610,000 adults in the U.S alone also died from some form of cardiovascular disease!

Now those are not small numbers to scoff at, and believe it or not, amongst some different factors, HIGH sodium intake is one of the culprits causing all of these issues!

Therefore, I do believe that it is high that we take a stand against this and try and learn how to lead a better and healthy life.

The first few chapters, therefore, focus on the basics of Low Sodium Diet and explain the requirements as settled by the American Heart Association. The remaining chapters focus on providing you amazing Low Sodium recipes that you can easily enjoy with a peace of mind.

Thank you for downloading and purchasing this book, I hope that you will find the information useful.

Stay healthy and God Bless!

Chapter 1: The Basics of Low Sodium Diet

So before going into the recipes themselves, let's start with the fundamentals of the diet first.

Sodium vs. Salt

To start off the chapter, let's begin by explaining the core difference between "Sodium" and "Salt" because it seems that almost every now and then, people seem to confuse these two and interchange while using them.

Now, you should know that both of them are referring to entirely different things.

Sodium is the sixth most abundant element found on earth and is naturally found in the earth and the environment. It is mostly bound up in minerals and rocks and is mined and further refined for later use.

This is a "Component" of the general table salt that we consume.

To break it down, Table salt contains about 60% Chloride and 40% Sodium.

Hence, a proper name for table salt would be "NaCl," or "Sodium Chloride."

Some people often consider that table salt is the only source of sodium. However, that's far from the truth.

Various other ingredients also contain a significant amount of Sodium that we often forget. So, even if you are not consuming raw salt, you are still exposing yourself to sodium even while you are eating boiled eggs!

Risk of high sodium intake

You have definitely heard people saying that "Too much sodium will damage your health" right?

Well, that's true, but let me explain to you exactly "How" it's going to impact your health negatively.

Cardiovascular Symptoms

Too much sodium will inevitably lead to high blood pressure and fluid retention in the body. These two factors work together to make the heart work harder and pump more blood, which again increases your overall blood pressure further.

This puts a lot of strain on your Heart and dramatically increases the risk of heart failures and stroke.

Impact on Bones

Too much salt increases the amount of calcium lost through urine, and Chronic loss of calcium increases your chances of suffering from osteoporosis.

For those of you who don't know, Osteoporosis is a condition where your bone mass diminishes, and they become increasingly fragile.

Impact on Kidneys

Consuming too much sodium negatively impacts your kidney as well! The increased level of urinary calcium increases the risk of kidney stones.

Not only that, but high sodium has also been seen to defer the proper functioning of kidneys and may ultimately lead to kidney failure.

Cancer

According to recent research done by the American Institute for Cancer Research and The World Cancer Research Fund, high intake of sodium and/or salty food have been seen to significantly increase the risk of stomach cancer, as they can harm the stomach linings.

The basics of low sodium diet according to American Heart Association.

Generally speaking, a Low Sodium diet is a diet that restricts the intake of sodium found in table salt and other sodium-rich foods.

This diet works even better when you combine it with the baselines presented by the American Heart Association.

According to the data found on "Guidelines on Lifestyle Management to Reduce Cardiovascular Risk," it is seen that the American Heart Association recommends that you try to trim down your sodium intake by following a dietary pattern that focuses mostly on the consumption of fruits, vegetables, whole grains, etc.

This means you should go for low-fat dairy products, poultry, legumes, fish, non-tropical vegetable oils and nuts and significantly limit your intake of sodium, sweets, red meats and sugar-sweetened beverages.

To be more precise, the dietary requirement recommends:

- You limit your saturated fat intake to 5-6% of total calorie intake
- Lower down the % of calories from trans-fat and saturated fat

- Keep sodium intake below 2,300mg per day.

- Keep the sodium intake below 1,500mg per day for individuals who are suffering from/or want to prevent pre-hypertension, hypertension, cardiovascular diseases and so on.

- Limit the intake of added sugar to less than 10% of total calories per day.

What to eat and what to avoid

That being said, here is a list of the foods and ingredients that you should keep an eye out for.

High-Sodium Foods:

- Frozen Breaded meats such as pizza, burritos
- Salted nuts
- Canned beans with salt
- Canned entrees such as spam, chili or ravioli
- Smoked, salted, cured, canned or any processed meat
- Buttermilk
- Regular/Processed cheese, sauces and cheese spread
- Cottage cheese
- Bread rolls, salted tops
- Quick bread, biscuits, self-rising flour, waffle mix, pancakes
- Pizza, salted crackers, croutons
- Pre-packaged mixes for rice, pasta, potatoes, etc.
- Canned vegetables
- Olives, pickles, sauerkraut and other pickled vegetables

- Veggies made with bacon, salted pork or ham

- Commercially prepared pasta and tomato sauces

- Regular canned/dehydrated soup, bouillon, broth

- Cup noodles/ ramen mixes

- Soy sauce, seasoning salt, etc.

- Bottled salad dressing

- Salted butter

- Instant cake or pudding mix

- Large portion of ketchup or mustard

Low Sodium Alternatives:

- Frozen/Fresh beef, pork, poultry, fish or lamb

- Low Sodium Peanut Butter

- Eggs and Egg Substitute

- Dry Peas and Beans

- Milk, ice cream, ice milk

- Low Sodium cheese, ricotta cheese, cream cheese, mozzarella

- Breads, rolls and bagels with no salted tops

- Muffins and most cereals

- All rice, pasta (make sure not to add salt while cooking)

- Low sodium corn and flour tortillas/noodles

- Low sodium crackers, breadsticks

- Unsalted popcorns, pretzels and chips

- Low sodium canned/dehydrated soups, broth, bouillon

- Homemade soup with no salt

- Vinegar, unsalted butter, margarine

- Vegetable oil and low sodium sauces, salad dressings
- Mayonnaise
- Fresh vegetables, without sauce
- Low sodium canned veggies
- Fresh potatoes
- Low salt tomato juice
- Most fresh/frozen fruits
- Dried fruits
- Dessert made without salt

Advantages of Low-Sodium Diet

Following a low Sodium Diet comes with a plethora of benefits!

Since you will go on a healthy food spree, the following benefits will also bless you!

- Helps to lower down cholesterol levels
- Aids in weight loss (discussed later)
- Gives you a healthier heart
- Helps to prevent Osteoporosis
- Helps to improve Kidney health
- Helps to prevent cancer
- Helps to control Diabetes
- Helps to avoid depression

And those are just the tip of the iceberg!

A note on salt alternatives

If you ever find yourself stuck with a recipe that asks for salt, you may look at the following alternatives that are amazing for converting your salty recipe to a low sodium one!

Sunflower Seeds

Sunflower seeds are fantastic salt alternatives, and they give a sweet nutty and slightly sweet flavor. You may use the seeds raw or roasted.

Fresh Squeezed Lemon

Lemon is believed to be a nice hybrid between citron and bitter orange. These are packed with Vitamin C, which helps to neutralize damaging free radicals from the system.

Onion Powder

For those of you who don't know, Onion powder is a dehydrated and ground spice that is made out of onion bulb. The powder is mostly used for seasoning in many spices! Keep in mind that onion powder and onion salt are two different things.

We are using onion powder here. They sport a nice mix of sweet, spice and bit an earthy flavor.

Black Pepper Powder

The black pepper powder is also a salt alternative that is native to India. You may use them by grinding whole peppercorns!

Cinnamon

Cinnamon is a very popular and savory spice that comes from the inner bark of trees. Two varieties of cinnamon include Ceylon and Chinese, and they sport a sharp, warm and sweet flavor.

Flavored Vinegar

Fruit infused vinegar or flavored vinegar as we call in our book are mixtures of vinegar that is combined with fruits to give a sweet flavor. These are excellent ingredients to add a bit of flavor to meals without salt. Experimentation might be required to find the perfect fruit blend for you.

As for the process of making the vinegar:

- Wash your fruits and slice them well
- Place ½ a cup of your fruit in a mason jar
- Top them up with white wine vinegar (or balsamic vinegar)
- Allow them to sit for 2 weeks or so
- Strain and use as needed

Some healthy oil

Commonly you can use olive oil as your go-to oil in the Low Sodium diet. However, there are some pretty good alternatives as well that you should know about.

Coconut Oil: When it comes to high heat cooking, coconut oil is the best with over 90 of the fatty acids being saturated, which makes it very resistant to heat. This particular oil is semi-solid at room temperature and can be used for months without it turning rancid.

This particular oil also has a lot of health benefits! Since this oil is rich in a fatty acid known as Lauric Acid, it can help to improve cholesterol levels and kill various pathogens.

Extra-Virgin Olive Oil: Olive oil is very well known for the heart health benefits. Some recent studies have shown that olive oil can even help to improve health biomarkers such as increasing the HDL cholesterol and lowering the amount of harmful LDL cholesterol.

Avocado Oil: The composition of Avocado oil is very similar to olive oil, and as such it holds same health benefits. It can be used for many purposes as an alternative for olive oil (Such as cooking).

Fish Oil: Fish oil is extremely rich in Omega-3 Fatty acids such as EPA and DHA. Just a tablespoon of Fish oil is enough to satisfy the body's daily fatty acids needs.

If you are looking for the best fish oil, then Cod Fish Liver Oil is your best option, which is also rich in Vitamin D3.

Grapeseed Oil: Grapeseed Oil is a very versatile form of cooking oil that is extracted from grape seeds left over from winemaking. This is very favorite oil amongst chefs and foodies! This oil has a very mild flavor that can be added with other ingredients that give a robust flavor to meals.

Grapeseed has a very high percentage of polyunsaturated fat and has a similar fatty acid profile to soybean oil.

According to multiple sources, Grapeseed oil has a good number of positive effects on the heart.

Chapter 2: Fantastic Tips for Your Low Sodium Diet

If you have gone through the chapter above, you are pretty much ready to jump into the Low-Sodium diet. However, the following tips and tricks prescribed by the American Heart Association will help you further elevate the positive impacts of your diet.

American Heart Association Recommended Tips for A Healthy Low Sodium Diet

Always read nutrition labels before buying food: People often tend to ignore the food labels printed on various ingredients and meals. But having a look at them is crucial when trying to maintain a proper low sodium diet.

High levels of sodium may seem hidden in pre-packaged food, especially when they don't taste salty at all!

In situations like these, the nutritional labeling will let you know if there are indeed any "Hidden" sodium contents.

Also, pay attention to the serving size as well.

Keep in mind that if you ever see a label where the sodium level is not indicated, but words such as LOW, HIGH... are used.

They mean:

- LOW indicates a sodium level of 120mg or less per serving
- HIGH suggests a sodium level of 480mg of more

- Very low indicates a sodium level of 35mg or less.

The Food and Drug Administration recommends going for as low as possible.

Always try to choose fresh fruits and vegetables: Generally speaking, fruits don't contain a lot of sodium.

Take an apple, orange or banana, for example, they hold only 1 mg of sodium! However, other fruits such as cantaloupe have 14 mg of sodium (which is still on the lower end of the spectrum).

Vegetables, on the other hand, have slightly higher sodium content. Avocado has about 10mgof Sodium, broccoli has about 12 mg, and spinach has about 22mg.

As you can see, all of these still fall way below harmful levels, so feel free to munch on them often!

Limit your processed food intake: It has been estimated that more than 75% of sodium consumed by Americans from Processed and junk foods!

Even if a processed food does not seem salty, rest assured that they are still packed with 9-10 times more sodium than regular counterparts.

Therefore, it is best to purchase ingredients as fresh as possible. And if you do end up buying canned goods, make sure to give the label a deep look.

Avoid adding salts while cooking and use herbs instead: Instead of using salts to flavor your meals, try going to olive oil or balsamic vinegar. Regarding potatoes/ pasta try using a variety of spices and instead of salting your eggs, use low sodium salsa!

This is a place where you are allowed to be as creative as you want and go wild with various herbs and spices.

Try to go for foods with potassium: Try to look for food that has a right amount of potassium as they help to lower down the harmful effects of sodium and improve your blood pressure condition.

Cooking Guidelines

The following cooking methods will also help you to trim down excess hidden sodium from your meals.

Steaming: This method will require you to place food in a perforated container and place it over simmering liquid. The heat from the steam cooks the food. Steaming helps retain the flavor of the food while cooking it and does not require any salt.

Poaching: Poaching is the technique of simmering your food over flavorful liquid such as low-sodium broth, vinegar, wine or plain water with some added herbs and spices.

Broiling/Grilling: Both of these techniques will require you to expose foods to direct heat. Both of these methods allow fat to drip away from the menu and are excellent from chicken, fruits, fish, and vegetables.

Stir-Frying: This is a traditional Asian method. Stir-frying quickly cooks small, uniformly cut pieces of food while they are rapidly stirred in a wok or large non-stick frying pan. You only need a little amount oil, and this is excellent for cooking red meat, fruits, chicken, fish, pork, veggies and so on. The final result is delicious as well.

Roasting: Roasting uses an oven's dry heat to cook food! This method is similar to baking but is done at a much higher temperature. Foods can be roasted in baking sheets or roasting pans and are suitable for poultry, seafood, and meats. You may place them on a rack in the roasting pan to allow the fat to drip away.

Sautéing: Sautéing usually involves the use of non-stick pan with little to no oil. This method quickly cooks relatively thin/small pieces of red meat, fish, fruits, chicken or vegetables.

Chapter 3: A Note on Instant Pot

Recent technological achievements have given birth to some of the most awesome culinary appliances to date!

You have your Air Fryer, Slow Cookers, Crock Pots, Sous Vide Circulators...the list goes on!

Following that tradition, the Instant Pot was introduced to the world with a very bold intention of being the "One Pot to Rule Them All".

As it turns out, the versatility of the Instant Pot actually helped it to receive that title!

So, the Instant Pot is a device that allows users to seamlessly harness the power of pressure cooking and cook their meals within minutes!

And the best part of the pot is the fact that unlike regular Pressure Cookers, the pot will allow you to make pretty much anything you can think of!

Cakes, Poultry, Vegetables, Red Meat...The Instant Pot is designed to handle them all!

As for the science behind the concept, well...

Pressure Cooking is generally the process of cooking meal inside a sealed-up vessel by trapping or generating steam inside of it.

Instant Pot's tend to work following the same principle.

Simply put the boiling point of water increases as the pressure increases.

When it comes an Instant Pot, as more and more steam is being generated inside, the pressure eventually increases. This leads to the water reaching very high temperatures without actually boiling up or evaporating which helps the device to greatly minimize the time taken to prepare the meals.

A brief look at the buttons of the Instant Pot

As mentioned above, in the previous section, the pot comes packed with a great number of different pre-programmed options to make cooking a delight.

However, due to the large number of available options, people sometimes tend to get confused and overwhelmed! An easy way to avoid this is to have a proper understanding of the buttons.

This particular section is dedicated towards helping you to understand what each button does and how you can use them to cook your masterpiece.

- Sauté: You should go for this button if you want to simply sauté your vegetables or produces inside your inner pot while keeping the lid opened. It is possible to adjust the level of brownness you desire by pressing the adjust button as well. As a small tip here, you can very easily press the Sauté Button followed by the Adjust Button two times to simmer your food.

- Keep Warm/Cancel: Using this button, you will be able to turn your pressure cooker off. Alternatively, you can use the adjust button to keep maintaining a warm temperature ranging from 145-degree Celsius (at normal) to 167 (at more) degree Celsius depending on what you need.

- Manual: This is pretty much an all-rounder button which gives a greater level of flexibility to the user. Using this button followed by the + or – buttons, you will be able to set the exact duration of cooking time which you require.

- Soup: This mode will set the cooker to a high-pressure mode giving 30 minutes of cooking time (at normal); 40 minutes (at more); 20 minutes (at less)

- Meat/Stew: This mode will set the cooker to a high-pressure mode giving 35 minutes of cooking time (at normal); 45 minutes (at more); 20 minutes (at less)

- Bean/Chili: This mode will set the cooker to a high-pressure mode giving 30 minutes of cooking time (at normal); 40 minutes (at more); 25 minutes (at less)

- Poultry: This mode will set the cooker to a high-pressure mode giving 15 minutes of cooking time (at normal); 30 minutes (at more); 5 minutes (at less)

- Rice: This is a fully automated mode which cooks rice on low pressure. It will adjust the timer all by itself depending on the amount of water/rice present inside the inner cooking pot.

- Multi-Grain: This mode will set the cooker to a high-pressure mode giving 40 minutes of cooking time (at normal); 45 minutes (at more); 20 minutes (at less)

- Porridge: This mode will set the cooker to a high-pressure mode giving 20 minutes of cooking time (at normal); 30 minutes (at more); 15 minutes (at less)

- Steam: This will set your pressure cooker to high pressure with 10 minutes cooking time at normal. 15 minutes cook time at more and 3 minutes cook time at less. Keep in mind that it is advised to use this mode with a steamer basket or rack for best results.

- Slow Cooker: This button will normally set the cooker at 4-hour mode. However, you change the temperature by keeping it at 190-201-degree Fahrenheit (at low); 194-205-degree Fahrenheit (at normal); 199-210-degree Fahrenheit (at high);

- Pressure: This button allows you to alter between high and low-pressure settings.

- Yogurt: This setting should be used when you are in the mood for making yogurt in individual pots or jars

- Timer: This button will allow you to either decrease or increase the time by using the timer button and pressing the + or – buttons.

Advantages of using an Instant Pot

- Save both energy and time: Thanks to the pressure cooking process of the Instant Pot, foods are cooked almost 70% faster than other traditional cooking methods. This process uses much less water while cooking! Since the exterior of the pot is insulated, it greatly minimizes energy and heat loss, which altogether contributes to lower energy required to boil, cook or steam meals!
- Preserve the nutrients of the food while keeping things tasty: Unlike the other cooking methods out there, the Instant Pot just requires to have enough water to produce the steam required for the meal, instead of requiring the produces to be submerged completely. This helps to prevent the vitamins and all essential minerals from the vegetables and other produces to wash away.

- Kills of harmful Micro-Organism: Pressure cooker allows the internal temperature to reach extremely high levels where most bacteria and viruses are killed off. Even the tough to kill ones that are found on raw maize or corns.

The basics of using an Instant Pot

Regardless of what other people says, using an Instant Pot is actually extremely easy and anyone can master it within a minute.

However, before "How the meals are cooked" and "How the pressure is released"

Now one thing you should keep in mind is that the processes that are used in this book are known as "Water Test"

re using the pot there is two things that you should know about.

- Open up the lid of your Instant Pot
- Add 1 or 2 cups of water into the inner pot of your Instant Pot
- Gently, move the valve to sealing position

- Select your pressure cooker timing, just use the manual button to set it to 5 minutes
- And that's it! Now all you have to do is just wait until the timer runs out! Within 5 minutes, the water should be heated up enough to have produced a good level of pressure

Next comes the process of releasing the pressure.

There are actually two ways through which the pressure can be released.

- Quick Release: This method is best suited for situations when you are using ingredients such as veggies.
- Natural Release: This process will require to you wait for about 10 minutes to allow the pressure to vent out. This process is suitable for ingredients such as meat.

And with that you are now ready to dive into the recipes

Chapter 4: Breakfast Recipes

Artichoke Macaroni

Serving: 6

Prep Time: 5 minutes

Cook Time: 20 minutes

Ingredients

- 1 tablespoon olive oil
- 1 large onion, diced
- 10 garlic cloves, minced
- 14-ounce fresh artichoke hearts
- 1-pound uncooked macaroni shells
- 4 cups vegetable broth
- 1 teaspoon red pepper flakes
- 4 ounces mozzarella cheese
- ¼ cup cashew cream

How To

1. Set the pot to Sauté mode and add oil, allow the oil to heat up and add onions
2. Cook for 2 minutes
3. Add garlic and stir well
4. Add artichoke hearts and Sauté for 1 minute more
5. Add uncooked pasta and 3 cups of broth alongside 2 cups of water
6. Mix well
7. Lock up the lid and cook on HIGH pressure for 4 minutes
8. Quick release the pressure
9. Open the pot and stir
10. Add extra water and fold in spinach and cook on Sauté mode for a few minutes
11. Add cashew cream and grated vegan cheese

12. Add pepper flakes and mix well
13. Enjoy!

<u>Nutrition (Per Serving)</u>

- Calories: 649
- Fat: 29g
- Carbohydrates: 64g
- Protein: 34g

Early Morning Egg Risotto

Serving: 4

Prep Time: 10 minutes

Cook Time: 12 minutes

Ingredients

- 3 slices bacon, low sodium and chopped
- 1 cup white rice
- 1/3 cup yellow onion, chopped
- 1 and ½ cups low sodium chicken stock
- 2 eggs, fried
- 2 tablespoons low –fat parmesan, grated
- 1 tablespoons chives, chopped
- Pinch of black pepper

How To

1. Set your pot to Sauté mode and add bacon, stir cook for 2-3 minutes
2. Add onions and cook for 2 minutes more
3. Add rice, stock, parmesan, black pepper and stir
4. Close lid and cook on HIGH pressure for 7 minutes
5. Release pressure naturally over 10 minutes
6. Divide the mix between plates and top with eggs, sprinkle chives and serve
7. Enjoy!

Nutrition (Per Serving)

- Calories: 212
- Fat: 5g
- Carbohydrates: 19g
- Protein: 6g

Strawberry and Quinoa Delight

Serving: 4

Prep Time: 10 minutes

Cook Time: 4 minutes

Ingredients

- 1 and ½ cups quinoa
- 2 and ¼ cups water
- ½ teaspoon vanilla extract
- ½ teaspoon pumpkin pie extract
- 2 cups strawberries, sliced
- ½ cup non-fat yogurt

How To

1. Add quinoa, water, vanilla, pumpkin pie spice, strawberries and yogurt to your pot
2. Stir and close lid
3. Cook on HIGH pressure for 4 minutes
4. Release pressure naturally
5. Open lid and stir
6. Divide into bowls and serve, enjoy!

Nutrition (Per Serving)

- Calories: 171
- Fat: 2g
- Carbohydrates: 9g
- Protein: 4g

Subtle Chicken Pasta

Serving: 4

Prep Time: 2 minutes

Cook Time: 4 minutes

Ingredients

- 1-pound chicken breast, skinless and boneless, cut into bite sized portions
- 2 tablespoons olive oil
- 1 pack ranch dressing (low sodium)
- ¼ cup bacon, chopped
- 8-ounce cream cheese
- 1-pound dry penne pasta
- 3 cups low-sodium chicken broth
- 2 cups water
- 8-ounce mozzarella cheese

How To

1. Set your pot to Sauté mode and add oil, allow the oil to heat up
2. Add chicken and ranch pack, stir for 1-2 minutes
3. Add cream cheese, broth, pasta to the pot
4. Lock up the lid and cook on HIGH pressure for 4 minutes
5. Perform a quick release
6. Stir in cheese and cooked bacon
7. Warm for 5 minutes and serve!

Nutrition (Per Serving)

- Calories: 134
- Fat: 11g
- Carbohydrates: 3g
- Protein: 6g

Easy Going Vanilla Oats

Serving: 4

Prep Time: 10 minutes

Cook Time: 10 minutes

Ingredients

- 1 cup almond milk
- 2 and ½ cups water
- 1 cup old-fashioned oats
- 2 tablespoons coconut sugar
- 1 teaspoon espresso powder
- 2 teaspoons vanilla extract

How To

1. Add milk, oats, sugar, espresso, vanilla extract to your Pot and toss
2. Close lid and cook on HIGH pressure for 10 minutes
3. Release pressure naturally over 10 minutes
4. Stir and divide into serving bowls
5. Serve and enjoy!

Nutrition (Per Serving)

- Calories: 177
- Fat: 2g
- Carbohydrates: 10g
- Protein: 4g

Crazy Peach Oatmeal

Serving: 4

Prep Time: 10 minutes

Cook Time: 10 minutes

Ingredients

- 4 cups old-fashioned rolled oats
- 3 and ½ cups low-fat milk
- 3 and ½ cups water
- 1 teaspoon cinnamon powder
- 1/3 cup palm sugar
- 4 peaches, chopped

How To

1. Add oats, milk, cinnamon, peaches, sugar to your pot and toss
2. Stir and close lid
3. Cook on HIGH pressure for 10 minutes
4. Release pressure naturally over 10 minutes
5. Open lid and serve
6. Enjoy!

Nutrition (Per Serving)

- Calories: 192
- Fat: 3g
- Carbohydrates: 12g
- Protein: 4g

Generous Baked Eggs

Serving: 4

Prep Time: 10 minutes

Cook Time: 4 minutes

Ingredients

- 4 whole eggs
- 4 slices low-fat cheddar
- 2 spring onions, chopped
- 1 tablespoon olive oil
- 1 tablespoon cilantro, chopped
- 1 cup water

How To

1. Grease 4 ramekins with oil and sprinkle green onion in each
2. Crack an egg into each and top with cilantro and cheese
3. Add water to your pot
4. Place a steamer basket
5. Place ramekin inside and cover
6. Cook on LOW pressure for 4 minutes
7. Release pressure naturally
8. Serve and enjoy!

Nutrition (Per Serving)

- Calories: 211
- Fat: 3g
- Carbohydrates: 18g
- Protein: 5g

Just Deserving Peach Breakfast

Serving: 3

Prep Time: 10 minutes

Cook Time: 4 minutes

Ingredients

- 6 small peaches, cored and cut into wedges
- ¼ cup maple syrup
- 2 tablespoons almond butter
- ½ teaspoon almond extract

How To

1. Add peach wedges, maple syrup, butter, almond extract to your pot and toss
2. Close lid and cook on HIGH pressure for 4 minutes
3. Quick release the pressure
4. Divide mix in bowls and serve
5. Enjoy!

Nutrition (Per Serving)

- Calories: 188
- Fat: 2g
- Carbohydrates: 15g
- Protein: 7g

Chapter 5: Soups and Stews Recipes

Fancy Rich Beef Stew

Serving: 6

Prep Time: 10 minutes

Cook Time: 40 minutes

Ingredients

- 2 pounds beef roast, fat removed and cubed
- 4 carrots, cubed
- 2 celery stalks, chopped
- 1 yellow onion, chopped
- 2 tablespoons tapioca flour
- ½ cup tomato juice

How To

1. Add beef, carrots, celery, flour, onion and tomato juice to the pot and toss well
2. Close lid and cook on LOW pressure for 35 minutes
3. Release pressure naturally over 10 minutes
4. Open lid and divide into bowls
5. Serve and enjoy!

Nutrition (Per Serving)

- Calories: 261
- Fat :6g
- Carbohydrates: 18g
- Protein: 8g

Grand Ma's Carrot Soup

Serving: 4

Prep Time: 10 minutes

Cook Time: 15 minutes

Ingredients

- 10 whole carrots, chopped
- 3 garlic cloves, minced
- 1 yellow onion, chopped
- 14-ounce coconut milk
- 1 and a ½ cups of vegetable stock, low sodium
- 1 tablespoon of red curry paste
- 2 tablespoon of cilantro, chopped

How To

1. Add carrots, onion, garlic, milk, stock, curry paste, cilantro to your Instant Pot and toss well to combine them
2. Lock up the lid and cook on HIGH pressure for 15 minutes
3. Release the pressure naturally over 10 minutes
4. Blend using immersion blender
5. Transfer to bowls and enjoy!

Nutrition Values (Per Serving)

- Calories: 251
- Fat: 4g
- Carbohydrates: 18g
- Protein: 6g

Gold Hearted Fish Soup

Serving: 4

Prep Time: 10 minutes

Cook Time: 20 minutes

Ingredients

- 1 yellow onion, chopped
- 12 cups of low sodium chicken stock
- 1-pound carrots, sliced
- 1 tablespoon of olive oil
- Black pepper as needed
- 2 tablespoon of ginger, minced
- 1 cup of water
- 1 pound of white fish, skinless, boneless and cut into medium chunks

How To

1. Set your pot to Sauté mode and add oil, allow the oil to heat up
2. Add onion and stir cook for 4 minutes
3. Add water, stock, carrots, ginger and stir
4. Lock up the lid and cook on HIGH pressure for 8 minutes
5. Release the pressure naturally over 10 minutes
6. Blend the soup using immersion blender
7. Add fish and season with pepper
8. Lock up the lid and cook on HIGH pressure for 6 minutes
9. Perform a quick release
10. Ladle the soup into soup bowls and enjoy!

Nutrition Values (Per Serving)

- Calories: 261

- Fat: 6g
- Carbohydrates: 11g
- Protein: 9g

Lovely Butternut Soup

Serving: 4

Prep Time: 5 minutes

Cook Time: 30 minutes

Ingredients

For Soup

- 1 teaspoon of extra virgin olive oil
- 1 large onion, chopped
- 2 garlic cloves, minced
- 1 tablespoon of curry powder
- 3 pound of butternut squash, cut up into 1-inch cubes and peeled
- 3 cups of water
- ½ a cup of coconut milk

For Extra Toppings

- Hulled up pumpkin seeds
- Dried up cranberries

How To

1. Set the pot to Sauté mode and add olive oil
2. Allow the oil to heat up and add onions, Sauté them for 8 minutes
3. Add garlic, curry powder and Sauté for 1 minute
4. Cancel Sauté mode and add butternut squash and water
5. Lock up the lid and cook for 30 minutes at HIGH pressure
6. Release the pressure naturally
7. Open the lid and blend the mixture using an immersion blender
8. Stir in coconut milk and season well
9. Serve with a topping of cranberries or pumpkin seeds

Nutrition Values (Per Serving)

- Calories: 124
- Fat: 6g
- Carbohydrates: 18g
- Protein: 2g

Creative Cabbage and Leek Soup

Serving: 4

Prep Time: 10 minutes

Cook Time: 25 minutes

Ingredients

- 2 tablespoon coconut oil
- ½ head cabbage, chopped
- 3-4 celery ribs, diced
- 2-3 leeks, cleaned and chopped
- 1 bell pepper, diced
- 2-3 carrots, diced
- 2-3 garlic cloves, minced
- 4 cups chicken broth
- 1 teaspoon Italian seasoning
- 1 teaspoon Creole seasoning
- Black pepper as needed
- 2-3 cups mixed salad greens

How To

1. Set your pot to Sauté mode and add coconut oil
2. Allow the oil to heat up
3. Add the veggies (except salad greens) starting from the carrot, making sure to stir it well after each vegetable addition
4. Make sure to add the garlic last
5. Season with Italian seasoning, black pepper and Creole seasoning
6. Add broth and lock up the lid
7. Cook on SOUP mode for 20 minutes

8. Release the pressure naturally and add salad greens, stir well and allow it to sit for a while

9. Allow for a few minutes to wilt the veggies

10. Season with a bit of flavored vinegar and pepper and enjoy!

Nutrition Values (Per Serving)

- Calories: 32
- Fat: 0g
- Carbohydrates: 4g
- Protein: 2g

Spicy Butternut Stew

Prep Time: 10 minutes

Cooking Time: 15 minutes

Serving: 6

Ingredients

- 3 cups of vegetable broth
- 2 cups of butternut squash
- 2 cups of kidney beans, cooked
- 1 cup yellow onion, chopped
- 1 cup of yellow corn kernels
- 2 garlic cloves, minced
- 1 can have diced tomatoes
- 1 teaspoon of paprika
- 1 teaspoon of ground cumin
- 1/8 teaspoon of Ancho chili powder

How To

1. Add all of the listed ingredients to the pot
2. Lock up the lid and cook on HIGH pressure for 5 minutes
3. Release the pressure naturally
4. Remove the lid and allow it to cool
5. Enjoy!

Nutrition Values (Per Serving)

- Calories: 127
- Fat: 5g
- Carbohydrates: 20g
- Protein: 3g

Mouthwatering Cauliflower Soup

Serving: 4

Prep Time: 10 minutes

Cook Time: 15 minutes

<u>Ingredients</u>

- 1 yellow onion, chopped
- 2 teaspoon of olive oil
- 3 garlic cloves, minced
- 1-pound cauliflower florets
- 1-pound butternut squash, peeled and cubed
- 2 cups of vegetable stock, low sodium
- 1 teaspoon of sweet paprika
- ½ a teaspoon of red pepper flakes
- 1 teaspoon of thyme, dried
- ½ a cup of coconut milk

<u>How To</u>

1. Set your pot to Sauté mode and add oil, allow the oil to heat up
2. Add garlic and onion, stir cook for 1-2 minutes
3. Add cauliflower, stock, squash, paprika, pepper flakes and thyme
4. Toss well
5. Lock up the lid and cook on HIGH pressure for 15 minutes
6. Release the pressure naturally over 10 minutes
7. Remove lid and add coconut milk, blend using an immersion blender
8. Transfer the soup to serving bowls
9. Enjoy!

<u>Nutrition Values (Per Serving)</u>

- Calories: 271

- Fat: 7g
- Carbohydrates: 20g
- Protein: 6g

Chapter 6: Beans and Grains Recipes

Black Bean Rice

Serving: 2

Prep Time: 10 minutes

Cook Time: 45 minutes

Ingredients

- 1 cup brown rice
- ½ cup dry black beans
- 2 and ½ cup water
- ½ red onion, diced
- ½ red pepper, diced
- 2 garlic cloves, minced
- 1 teaspoon better than bouillon cubes
- 1 tablespoon chili powder
- ½ teaspoon cayenne pepper
- 1 teaspoon cumin

How To

1. Mince garlic
2. Dice the onions
3. Set your pot to Sauté mode and add the garlic and onions, Sauté for 5 minutes
4. Set your pot to WARM mode and add the remaining ingredients (Except pepper)
5. Lock up the lid and cook on HIGH pressure for 25 minutes
6. Release the pressure naturally over 10 minutes
7. Add diced red pepper and serve!

Nutrition (Per Serving)

- Calories: 190

- Fat: 1g
- Carbohydrates: 39g
- Protein: 7g

Lentil and Faro Supreme

Serving: 4

Prep Time: 5 minutes

Cook Time: 30 minutes

<u>Ingredients</u>

For Lentil

- ½ cup lentils
- 1 and ¼ cup water
- ½ teaspoon dried oregano
- ½ teaspoon medium chili powder
- ½ teaspoon dried basil
- ¼ teaspoon cumin powder
- ¼ teaspoon smoked paprika
- ¼ teaspoon onion powder
- ¼ teaspoon garlic powder
- ¼ teaspoon black pepper

For Farro

- ½ a cup of faro
- 1 cup of water
- ½ a teaspoon of Italian herbs
- ½ a teaspoon of onion powder

<u>How To</u>

1. Add ingredients listed under lentil to the pot
2. Place trivet on top of the lentils
3. Add faro ingredients to a stainless-steel bowl and place it on top of the trivet
4. Lock up the lid and cook on HIGH pressure for 12 minutes

5. Release the pressure naturally
6. Serve with veggies
7. Enjoy!

Nutrition Values (Per Serving)

- Calories: 350
- Fat: 19g
- Carbohydrates: 38g
- Protein: 12g

Easy Rice Pudding

Serving: 6

Prep Time: 10 minutes

Cook Time: 20 minutes

Ingredients

- 2 cups coconut milk
- 1 and ¼ cups water
- 1 cup basmati rice
- ½ cup maple syrup
- ¾ cup coconut cream
- 1 teaspoon vanilla extract

How To

1. Add coconut milk, water, rice, coconut cream, maple syrup, vanilla to the pot and toss well
2. Close lid and cook on HIGH pressure for 20 minutes
3. Release pressure naturally over 10 minutes
4. Serve and enjoy!

Nutrition (Per Serving)

- Calories: 1221
- Fat: 4g
- Carbohydrates: 15g
- Protein: 6g

Colorful Confetti Basmati

Serving: 4

Prep Time: 5 minutes

Cook Time: 5 minutes

Ingredients

- 1 tablespoon olive oil
- 1 medium onion, chopped
- 1 bell pepper, chopped
- 1 carrot, grated
- Water as needed
- 2 cups water
- ½ cup peas

How To

1. Set your pot to Sauté mode and add olive oil, allow the oil to heat up
2. Add onion and Sauté
3. Take pot and add bell pepper, grated carrots and pat them down
4. Keep adding water until you reach 3 cups mark
5. Add rice and peas to your Instant Pot
6. Add the vegetable mixture to the pot
7. Lock up the lid and cook on HIGH pressure for 3 minutes
8. Release the pressure naturally
9. Fluff the rice with fork and serve!

Nutrition Values (Per Serving)

- Calories: 270
- Fat: 6g
- Carbohydrates: 46g
- Protein: 6g

Heart Warming Chicken Porridge

Serving: 4

Prep Time: 60 minutes

Cook Time: 10-20 minutes

Ingredients

- 1 cup jasmine rice
- 1 pound steamed/cooked chicken legs
- 5 cups chicken broth
- 4 cups water
- 1 and ½ cups fresh ginger
- Green onions
- Cashew nuts, toasted

How To

1. Place the rice in your fridge and allow it to chill 1 hour prior to cooking
2. Take the rice out and add them to your Instant Pot
3. Pour broth and water
4. Lock up the lid and cook on PORRIDGE mode
5. Release the pressure naturally over 10 minutes
6. Open the lid
7. Remove the meat from the chicken legs and add the meat to your soup
8. Stir well over Sauté mode
9. Season with a bit of flavored vinegar and enjoy with a garnish of nuts and onion

Nutrition (Per Serving)

- Calories: 206
- Fat: 8g
- Carbohydrates: 8g
- Protein: 23g

Fast-Forward Peruvian Dish

Serving: 3

Prep Time: 1 minute

Cook Time: 1 minute

<u>Ingredients</u>

- 1 cup of well rinsed quinoa
- 1 zested and squeeze lime
- Seasonal vegetables of your choosing

<u>How To</u>

1. Add quinoa, zest, water to your pot
2. Lock up the lid and cook on HIGH pressure for 1 minute
3. Once done, release the pressure naturally
4. Mix in lime juice and alongside additional seasoning
5. Mix in your desire veggies and serve!

<u>Nutrition Values (Per Serving)</u>

- Calories: 321
- Fat: 5g
- Carbohydrates: 38g
- Protein: 32g

Amazing Brown Rice

Serving: 4

Prep Time: 5 minutes

Cook Time: 22 minutes

Ingredients

- 2 cups brown rice
- 2 and ½ cups water

How To

1. Add rice to the Instant Pot
2. Add water and lock up the lid
3. Cook on HIGH pressure for 22 minutes
4. Release the pressure naturally and enjoy with your favorite dish!

Nutrition (Per Serving)

- Calories: 172
- Fat: 1g
- Carbohydrates: 36g
- Protein: 4g

Authentic Parmesan Chicken Spaghetti Squash

Serving: 4

Prep Time: 5 minutes

Cook Time: 20 minutes

Ingredients

- 1 spaghetti squash
- 1 cup Marinara sauce
- 1-pound cooked chicken, cubed
- 16-ounce mozzarella

How To

1. Split up the squash in halves and remove the seeds
2. Add 1 cup of water to the pot and place a trivet on top
3. Add the squash halves on the trivet
4. Lock up the lid and cook for 20 minutes at HIGH pressure
5. Do a quick release
6. Remove the squashes and shred them using a fork into spaghetti portions
7. Pour sauce over the squash and give it a nice mix
8. Top them up with the cubed-up chicken and top with mozzarella
9. Broil for 1-2 minutes and broil until the cheese has melted

Nutrition (Per Serving)

- Calories: 237
- Fats: 10g
- Carbs:32g
- Protein:11g

Chapter 7: Meatless Mains Recipes

The Marriage of Ginger and Butternut Squash

Serving: 8

Prep Time: 10 minutes

Cook Time: 15 minutes

<u>Ingredients</u>

- 2 pounds of butternut squash, peeled and chopped
- 2 whole eggs
- 2 cups of water
- 1 cup of coconut milk
- 2 tablespoon of coconut sugar
- 1 teaspoon of cinnamon powder
- ½ a teaspoon of ginger powder

<u>How To</u>

1. Add 1 cup of water to your Instant Pot
2. Add steamer basket and add squash pieces
3. Lock up the lid and cook on HIGH pressure for 5 minutes
4. Perform a quick release and remove the lid
5. Drain the cubes and transfer them to a bowl
6. Add sugar, milk, cinnamon, eggs and ginger and mash the whole mixture, whisk well
7. Pour the mixture into ramekins
8. Add remaining water to your Instant Pot
9. Place steamer basket and add the ramekins
10. Lock up the lid and cook on HIGH pressure for 14 minutes
11. Release the pressure naturally over 10 minutes
12. Serve and enjoy!

<u>Nutrition Values (Per Serving)</u>

- Calories: 182
- Fat: 1g
- Carbohydrates: 18g
- Protein: 3g

Glamorous Bell Pepper Stir Fry

Serving: 2

Prep Time: 5 minutes

Cook Time: 15 minutes

Ingredients

- 1 tablespoon of oil
- 2 bell peppers, cut into long pieces
- 4 baby potatoes
- ½ teaspoon cumin seeds
- 4 garlic cloves
- ½ a teaspoon of dry mango
- Cilantro for garnish

Spice

- 1.4 teaspoon of turmeric
- ½ a teaspoon of cayenne
- 2 teaspoons of coriander

How To

1. Set the pot to Sauté mode and add oil, allow the oil to heat up
2. Add garlic and cumin
3. Add cut bell pepper, spices, potatoes and mix well
4. Sprinkle water
5. Lock up the lid and cook on HIGH pressure for 2 minutes
6. Once done, release the pressure naturally
7. Stir in dry mango powder and lemon juice
8. Mix well and garnish with a bit of cilantro
9. Enjoy!

Nutrition Values (Per Serving)

- Calories: 333
- Fat: 24g
- Carbohydrates: 11g
- Protein: 18g

Smokey Sweet Black-Eyed Peas and Greens

Serving: 4

Prep Time: 1 minute

Cook Time: 20 minutes

<u>Ingredients</u>

- 1 teaspoon of oil
- 1 thinly sliced onion
- 2-3 garlic cloves, minced
- 1 cup red pepper, diced
- 1 hot Chile jalapeno
- 1-2 teaspoon of chili powder
- 1 and a ½ cup of black eyed peas, dried and soaked
- 4 dates, chopped
- 1 cup of water
- 1 can of fire roasted tomatoes
- 2 cups of greens, chopped
- Crushed Sunflower Seeds to Taste

<u>How To</u>

1. Set the pot to Sauté mode and add onion and Sauté for a few minutes
2. Add garlic and pepper and Sauté for 1 minute more
3. Add smoked paprika, chili powder, peas and dates
4. Stir well
5. Add water and stir
6. Lock up the lid and cook on HIGH pressure for 3 minutes
7. Release the pressure naturally and add tomatoes
8. Lock up the lid and let it sit for 5 minutes
9. Open the lid and adjust seasoning
10. Serve!

Nutrition Values (Per Serving)

- Calories: 108
- Fat: 3g
- Carbohydrates: 18g
- Protein: 4g

Yellow Split Pea Curry

Serving: 4

Prep Time: 5 minutes

Cook Time: 15 minutes

Ingredients

- ½ a cup of yellow split peas
- 2 and a ¼ cup of vegetable stock
- 1 tablespoon of nutritional yeast
- ¾ teaspoon of curry powder
- ½ a teaspoon of Italian herbs
- ½ a teaspoon of cumin
- ½ a teaspoon of onion powder
- ½ a teaspoon of crushed sunflower seeds
- ¼ teaspoon of garlic powder
- ¼ teaspoon of smoked paprika
- ¼ teaspoon of chili powder

How To

1. Add the listed ingredients to the pot
2. Lock up the lid and cook on HIGH pressure for 15 minutes
3. Release the pressure naturally
4. Serve over rice or quinoa
5. Enjoy!

Nutrition Values (Per Serving)

- Calories: 323
- Fat: 15g
- Carbohydrates: 36g
- Protein: 13g

Chapter 8: Chicken Recipes

Amazing Braised Chicken Drumsticks

Serving: 6

Prep Time: 10 minutes

Cook Time: 20 minutes

<u>Ingredients</u>

- 6 chicken drumsticks
- 1 tablespoon cider vinegar
- 1 teaspoon flavored vinegar
- 1/8 teaspoon black pepper
- 1 teaspoon dried oregano
- 1 teaspoon olive oil
- 1 and ½ cups tomatillo sauce
- ¼ cup cilantro, chopped
- 1 jalapeno, halved and seeded

<u>How To</u>

1. Season the chicken with vinegar, pepper, flavored vinegar and oregano
2. Allow it to marinate for a few hours
3. Set your pot to Sauté mode and add oil, allow the oil to heat up
4. Add chicken and brown it for about 4 minutes
5. Add cilantro, jalapeno and salsa
6. Cover the lid and cook on HIGH pressure for 20 minutes until the chicken is tender
7. Release the pressure naturally
8. Garnish with a bit of cilantro and serve!

<u>Nutrition (Per Serving)</u>

- Calories: 161

- Fat: 5g
- Carbohydrates: 5g
- Protein: 22g

Mamma Mia Italian Chicken

Serving: 4

Prep Time: 10 minutes

Cook Time: 15 minutes

Ingredients

- 1 tablespoon olive oil
- Pinch of black pepper
- 2 pounds chicken breasts, skinless, boneless and cubed
- 4 garlic cloves, minced
- 2 and ½ cups low-sodium chicken stock
- 2 cups coconut cream
- Pinch of nutmeg, ground
- ½ cup low-fat parmesan, grated
- 1 tablespoon basil, chopped

How To

1. Set your pot to Sauté mode and add oil, allow the oil to heat up
2. Add chicken cubes and brown for 2-3 minutes
3. Add garlic, stock, cream, nutmeg and toss well
4. Close lid and cook on HIGH pressure for 12 minutes
5. Release the pressure naturally over 10 minutes
6. Open lid and add cheese and basil
7. Toss well and serve

Nutrition (Per Serving)

- Calories: 261
- Fat: 6g
- Carbohydrates: 19g
- Protein: 7g

The Big Man's Chicken Zoodles

Serving: 4

Prep Time: 5 minutes

Cook Time: 22 minutes

<u>Ingredients</u>

- 1 and ½ pounds chicken thighs, boneless and skinless
- 1 and ½ tablespoon clarified butter
- 2 cups leeks, sliced
- 2 tablespoon apple cider vinegar
- ½ cup carrots, sliced
- 4 garlic cloves, minced
- 1 tablespoon great lakes beef gelatin
- ½ cup nutritional yeast
- ½ teaspoon flavored vinegar
- 1 teaspoon Italian herb mix (rosemary, basil, oregano, sage etc.)
- 2 large zucchinis
- 1 bunch of broccoli rabe
- Fistful of mixed greens
- Extra clarified butter

<u>How To</u>

1. Set your pot to Sauté mode and add ghee, allow the ghee to heat up
2. Add carrots, leeks and garlic
3. Sauté for a while and add vinegar alongside herbs, chicken, yeast, beef gelatin
4. Stir well and lock up the lid
5. Set your pot to POULTRY mode and cook for 25 minutes
6. Spiralize the zucchini into zoodles and season with flavored vinegar
7. Cover them with a towel and keep them on the side
8. Mince a few garlic cloves

9. Dice up the broccoli and Sauté in a skillet over high heat (in ghee)
10. Stir well
11. Turn off the heat and add the greens
12. Mix well
13. Season with some flavored vinegar
14. Once the chicken is done, release the pressure naturally and remove the chicken
15. Shred the chicken using fork and allow it to cool (the veggies in the pot as well)
16. Add the zoodles and the broccoli mix to a bowl
17. Spoon the chicken over the veggies and serve altogether!

Nutrition (Per Serving)

- Calories: 205
- Fat: 12g
- Carbohydrates: 14g
- Protein: 14g

Traditional Chinese Chicken

Serving: 4

Prep Time: 10 minutes

Cook Time: 15 minutes

Ingredients

- 5 pounds chicken thighs
- Black pepper as needed
- ½ cup balsamic vinegar
- 1 teaspoon black peppercorns
- 4 garlic cloves, minced
- ½ cup coconut amino

How To

1. Add chicken, vinegar, amino, garlic, pepper, peppercorns to your pot and stir
2. Close lid and cook on HIGH pressure for 15 minutes
3. Release pressure naturally over 10 minutes
4. Serve and enjoy!

Nutrition (Per Serving)

- Calories: 261
- Fat: 7g
- Carbohydrates: 18g
- Protein: 8g

Genuine Cashew Chicken

Serving: 6

Prep Time: 3 minutes

Cook Time: 15 minutes

<u>Ingredients</u>

- 2 pounds chicken thigh, bones and skin removed
- ¼ teaspoon black pepper
- ¼ cup coconut amino
- 2 tablespoons rice vinegar
- 2 tablespoons of ketchup
- 1 tablespoon brown sugar
- 1 clove garlic, minced
- 1 teaspoon grated ginger
- 1 tablespoon arrowroot + 2 tablespoon water
- 1/3 cup cashew nuts, toasted
- ¼ cup green onions, chopped
- 2 tablespoons sesame seeds, toasted

<u>How To</u>

1. Add all of the ingredients to your Instant Pot (except cornstarch slurry, cashew, green onions, sesame seeds)
2. Gently stir
3. Lock lid and cook on HIGH pressure for 15 minutes
4. Quick release the pressure
5. Set your pot to Sauté mode and stir in slurry
6. Simmer until the sauce thickens
7. Stir in cashew nuts, green onions and sesame seeds
8. Serve and enjoy!

<u>Nutrition (Per Serving)</u>

- Calories: 444
- Fat: 32g
- Carbohydrates: 10g
- Protein: 27g

Chicken and Barley Mix

Serving: 4

Prep Time: 15 minutes

Cook Time: 55 minutes

Ingredients

- 6 ounces barley
- 5 ounces peas
- 1-pound chicken thigh
- 3 yellow onion, chopped
- 5 carrots, chopped
- 6 ounces veggie stock, low sodium
- 12 ounces water
- Black pepper as needed

How To

1. Add stock, water, barley to your pot
2. Close lid and cook on HIGH pressure for 20 minutes
3. Quick release pressure
4. Add onions, carrots, peas, chicken and stir
5. Cover and cook on HIGH pressure for 15 minutes
6. Season with black pepper and stir
7. Divide into bowls and serve
8. Enjoy!

Nutrition (Per Serving)

- Calories: 261
- Fat: 7g
- Carbohydrates: 18g
- Protein: 7g

Easy Going Sesame Chicken

Serving: 4

Prep Time: 10 minutes

Cook Time: 25 minutes

Ingredients

- 4 chicken breasts, skinless and boneless
- Pinch of black pepper
- ½ cup yellow onions, chopped
- ½ cup coconut amino
- ¼ cup no-salt tomato sauce
- 2 tablespoons avocado oil
- 2 garlic cloves, minced
- ¼ teaspoon red pepper flakes
- 1 teaspoon sesame seeds

How To

1. Add chicken, pepper, onion, tomato sauce, amino, garlic, oil, pepper flakes, sesame seeds to your pot and toss well
2. Lock lid and cook on HIGH pressure for 20 minutes
3. Release pressure naturally over 10 minutes
4. Transfer chicken to cutting board and shred using 2 forks
5. Return to pot and set your pot to Sauté mode
6. Cook for 5 minutes more

Nutrition (Per Serving)

- Calories: 251
- Fat: 4g
- Carbohydrates: 15g
- Protein: 7g

Chapter 9: Red Meat and Seafood Recipes

Garlic and Butter Sword Fish

Serving: 4

Prep Time: 10 minutes

Cook Time: 2 hours 30 minutes

Ingredients

- 5 sword fish fillets
- ½ cup melted butter
- 6 garlic cloves, chopped
- 1 tablespoon black pepper

How To

1. Take a mixing bowl and toss in all of your garlic, black pepper alongside the melted butter
2. Take a parchment paper and place your fish fillet in that paper
3. Cover it up with the butter mixture and wrap up the fish
4. Repeat the process until all of your fish are wrapped up
5. Let it cook for 2 and a half hours and release the pressure naturally
6. Serve

Nutrition (Per Serving)

- Calories: 379
- Fat: 26g
- Carbohydrates: 1g
- Protein: 34g

Easy Simple Lobster

Serving: 4

Prep Time: 10 minutes

Cook Time: 7 minutes

Ingredients

- 2 lobsters
- 1 cup water
- 1 cup white wine
- Melted butter for serving

How To

1. Add the listed ingredients to your Instant Pot
2. Close lid and cook on HIGH pressure for 7 minutes
3. Quick release the pressure
4. Open lid and add melted butter
5. Serve and enjoy!

Nutrition (Per Serving)

- Calories: 231
- Fat: 9g
- Carbohydrates: 5g
- Protein: 30g

Balsamic Beef Treat

Serving: 8

Prep Time: 5 minutes

Cook Time: 55 minutes

Ingredients

- 3 pounds chuck roast
- 3 garlic cloves, sliced
- 1 tablespoon oil
- 1 teaspoon flavored vinegar
- ½ teaspoon pepper
- ½ teaspoon rosemary
- 1 tablespoon butter
- ½ teaspoon thyme
- ¼ cup balsamic vinegar
- 1 cup beef broth

How To

1. Cut slits in the roast and stuff garlic slices
2. Take a bowl and add vinegar, pepper, rosemary, thyme, pepper
3. Rub the mixture all over
4. Set your pot to Sauté mode and add oil
5. Add roast and brown both sides (5 minutes per side0
6. Take roast out and keep it on the side
7. Add butter, broth, balsamic vinegar and deglaze the pot
8. Transfer roast back to the pot and lock lid
9. Cook on HIGH pressure for 40 minutes
10. Quick release pressure
11. Remove lid and serve
12. Enjoy!

Nutrition (Per Serving)

- Calories: 393
- Fat: 15g
- Carbohydrates: 25g
- Protein: 37g

Generic Pressure-Cooked Crab Legs

Serving: 4

Prep Time: 5 minutes

Cook Time: 7 minutes

Ingredients

- 3 pounds crab legs
- 1 cup water
- 1 cup white wine
- 1 cup melted butter
- 1 lemon, sliced in wedges

How To

1. Add water and wine to your Instant Pot
2. Add crab legs
3. Close lid and cook on HIGH pressure for 7 minutes
4. Quick release the pressure
5. Open lid and add melted butter and a dash of lemon
6. Enjoy!

Nutrition (Per Serving)

- Calories: 191
- Fat: 1g
- Carbohydrates: 0g
- Protein: 41g

Awesome Shrimp Pasta

Serving: 4

Prep Time: 10 minutes

Cook Time: 6 minutes

Ingredients

- 2 pounds shrimp
- 2 tablespoons oil
- 2 tablespoons butter
- 1 tablespoon garlic, minced
- ½ cup white wine
- ½ cup chicken stock
- Cooked pasta (don't use salt)
- 1 tablespoon lemon juice
- Parsley for garnish
- Pepper as needed
- Flavored vinegar as needed

How To

1. Set the pot to Sauté mode and add oil and butter and allow to heat up
2. Add garlic and Sauté
3. Add white wine and chicken stock, stir
4. Cancel the Sauté mode and add shrimp
5. Lock up the lid and cook on MEAT/STEW mode for 1 minute
6. Naturally release the pressure over 5 minutes
7. Stir in cooked pasta and lemon juice, vinegar and pepper
8. Enjoy!

Nutrition (Per Serving)

- Calories: 355

- Fat: 15g
- Carbohydrates: 37g
- Protein: 17g

Pretty Pepper Steak

Serving: 4

Prep Time: 5 minutes

Cook Time: 20 minutes

Ingredients

- 1-pound boneless beef eye round steak
- 80 ounces mushrooms, sliced
- 1 red pepper, sliced
- 1 garlic, minced
- 1 pack onion soup mix
- 1 tablespoon sesame oil
- 1 cup water

How To

1. Add listed ingredients to your Pot
2. Close lid and cook on HIGH pressure for 20 minutes
3. Release pressure naturally
4. Serve and enjoy!

Nutrition (Per Serving)

- Calories: 222
- Fat: 15g
- Carbohydrates: 5g
- Protein: 36g

Cane Wrapped Prosciutto

Serving: 4

Prep Time: 2 minutes

Cook Time: 5 minutes

Ingredients

- 1-pound thick asparagus
- 80 ounces prosciutto, sliced

How To

1. Add 2 cups water to your pot
2. Take the asparagus and wrap them up in prosciutto spears.
3. Once all of the asparagus are wrapped, gently place the processed asparaguses in the cooking basket inside your pot in layers.
4. Turn up the heat to a high temperature and when there is a pressure build up, take down the heat and let it cook for about 2-3 minutes at the high pressure.
5. Once the timer runs out, gently open the cover of the pressure cooker
6. Take out the steamer basket from the pot instantly and toss the asparaguses on a plate to serve
7. Eat warm or let them come down to room temperature

Nutrition (Per Serving)

- Calories: 212
- Fat: 14g
- Carbohydrates: 11g
- Protein: 12g

Pork Loin Pear Chops

Serving: 4

Prep Time: 5 minutes

Cook Time: 12 minutes

Ingredients

- 2 tablespoon clarified butter
- 4 pieces ½ inch thick bone-In pork loin chops
- ½ teaspoon flavored vinegar
- ½ teaspoon ground black pepper
- 2 medium yellow onions, peeled and cut into 8 wedges
- 2 large Bosc pears, peeled and cored, cut into 4 wedges
- ½ cup unsweetened pear
- ½ teaspoon ground allspice
- Dash of hot pepper

How To

1. Set your pot to Sauté mode and add 1 tablespoon of butter, allow the butter to melt
2. Add chops and Sauté for 4 minutes
3. Transfer the chops to a plate and cook the remaining and brown them
4. Add onion and pears in the pot and allow them to Sauté for 3 minutes more until the pears are slightly browned
5. Pour cider and stir in allspice, pepper sauce
6. Nestle the chops back
7. Lock up the lid and cook on HIGH pressure for 10 minutes
8. Perform quick release
9. Serve over rice!

Nutrition (Per Serving)

- Calories: 318

- Fat: 19g
- Carbohydrates: 4g
- Protein: 31g

The Gamer Hunter's "Veal" Stew

Serving: 4

Prep Time: 10 minutes

Cook Time: 25 minutes

Ingredients

- 2 sprigs fresh rosemary
- 1 tablespoon olive oil
- 1 tablespoon butter
- 8 ounces shallots
- 2 carrot, chopped
- 2 stalks celery, chopped
- 2 tablespoons all-purpose flour
- 3 pounds veal
- Water
- 2 teaspoons flavored vinegar

How To

1. Set your pot to Sauté mode and add olive oil
2. Add butter, chopped rosemary, celery, shallots and sauté until you have a nice texture
3. Shove the veggies to the side and add meat cubes
4. Brown
5. Pour stock and cover the meat
6. Close lid and cook on HIGH pressure for 15-20 minutes
7. Release pressure naturally over 10 minutes
8. Open lid and set your pot to sauté mode
9. Simmer for 5 minutes
10. Serve and enjoy!

Nutrition (Per Serving)

- Calories: 470
- Fat: 22g
- Carbohydrates: 18g
- Protein: 47g

Lovely Salmon and Broccoli Mix

Serving: 4

Prep Time: 10 minutes

Cook Time: 4 minutes

Ingredients

- 2 and ½ ounces salmon fillets
- 2 and ½ ounces broccoli, chopped in florets
- 9 ounces new potatoes
- 1 teaspoon butter
- Pepper as needed
- Crushed sunflower seeds
- Fresh herbs

How To

1. Add ½ cup water to your Instant Pot
2. Season potatoes with sunflower seeds, fresh herb and pepper
3. Season salmon with broccoli florets and sunflower seeds and pepper
4. Add potatoes to steaming rack and smother with butter
5. Transfer to your pot
6. Lock lid and cook on STEAM for 2 minutes
7. Quick release
8. Add broccoli florets and salmon, close lid and STEAM cook for 2 minutes more
9. Quick release

Nutrition (Per Serving)

- Calories: 701
- Fat: 39g
- Carbohydrates: 30g
- Protein: 57g

Acorn Squash Ala Pork Chops

Serving: 6

Prep Time: 10 minutes

Cook Time: 10 minutes

Ingredients

- 2 tablespoons ghee
- 4 pieces 12-inch-thick bone-in pork chops
- ½ teaspoon flavored vinegar
- 2 medium acorn squash, peeled and deseeded, cut into eights
- 3 tablespoons dried sage
- ½ teaspoon dried thyme
- ½ teaspoon ground cinnamon
- ¾ cup chicken broth

How To

1. Set your pot to sauté mode and add 1 tablespoon butter
2. Season chops with pepper and flavored vinegar and add to the pot, cook for 4 minutes
3. Transfer chops to plate and repeat with the remaining chops
4. Add the chops back to the pot in a single layer
5. Add squash, sprinkle maple syrup, thyme, sage, cinnamon on top
6. Pour broth
7. Lock lid and cook on HIGH pressure for 10 minutes
8. Quick release pressure
9. Transfer chops to plate and serve

Nutrition (Per Serving)

- Calories: 348
- Fat: 18g
- Protein: 42g

Butter Pork Chops

Serving: 4

Prep Time: 5 minutes

Cook Time: 15 minutes

Ingredients

- 2 tablespoons butter
- 4 pieces ½ inch thick bone-in pork chops
- ½ teaspoon flavored butter
- ½ teaspoon ground black pepper
- 16 baby carrots
- 1 tablespoon fresh dill fronds, sliced
- ½ cup white wine
- ½ cup chicken broth (low sodium)

How To

1. Set your pot to sauté mode
2. Season the chops with pepper and flavored vinegar
3. Toss your chops into your pot and cook for 4 minutes
4. Transfer the chops to a plate and repeat to cook and brown the rest
5. Pour in 1 tablespoon of butter and Toss in your carrots, dill to the cooker and let it cook for about 1 minute
6. Pour in the wine and scrape off any browned bits in your cooker while the liquid comes to a boil
7. Stir in the broth
8. return the chops to your pot
9. Lock up the lid and let it cook for about 18 minutes at high pressure
10. Naturally release the pressure by keeping it aside for 8 minutes
11. Unlock and serve with some sauce poured over

Nutrition (Per Serving)

- Calories: 269
- Fat: 25g
- Carbohydrates: 0g
- Protein: 17g

Chapter 10: Dessert Recipes

Astonishing Cauliflower Mac and Cheese

Serving: 4

Prep Time: 5 minutes

Cook Time: 10 minutes

Ingredients

- 2 cups cauliflower rice
- 2 tablespoon cream cheese
- ½ cup half and half
- 1 teaspoon flavored vinegar
- 1 teaspoon fresh ground black pepper

How To

1. Take a heatproof bowl and add cauliflower, half and half, cream cheese, Cheddar cheese, flavored vinegar and mix well
2. Cover with aluminum foil
3. Pour 2 cups of water into the Instant Pot
4. Place a trivet
5. Place your heat proof bowl on top of the trivet
6. Lock up the lid and cook on HIGH pressure for 5 minutes
7. Release the pressure naturally over 10 minutes
8. Remove the bowl discard the foil
9. Place the cauliflower under broiler and broil for 3-5 minutes until the cheese is bubbly

Nutrition (Per Serving)

- Calories: 134
- Fat: 11g
- Carbohydrates: 3g

Coconut Figs Mix

Serving: 2

Prep Time: 6 minutes

Cook Time: 4 minutes

Ingredients

- 2 tablespoons fat-free coconut butter
- 12 figs, halved
- ¼ cup palm sugar
- 1 cup walnuts, toasted and chopped

How To

1. Add butter, figs, sugar, walnuts to your Instant Pot and toss
2. Close lid and cook on HIGH pressure for 4 minutes
3. Quick release pressure
4. Divide mix amongst serving bowls and serve
5. Enjoy!

Nutrition (Per Serving)

- Calories: 200
- Fat: 2g
- Carbohydrates: 12g
- Protein: 9g

Simple Plum Cake

Serving: 4

Prep Time: 10 minutes

Cook Time: 40 minutes

<u>Ingredients</u>

- 4 ounces plums, stoned removed and chopped
- 2 cups water
- 4 ounces apricot, chopped
- 1 cup flour
- 3 teaspoons baking powder
- 3 tablespoons coconut sugar
- 3 tablespoons avocado oil
- 3 tablespoons maple syrup
- 4 eggs
- 1 carrot, grated

<u>How To</u>

1. Add flour, baking powder, sugar to a blender and stir
2. Add oil, maple syrup, eggs, plums, carrots and apricots
3. Stir well and spread into a greased cake pan
4. Add water to the Instant Pot and add steamer
5. Add pudding, close lid and cook on HIGH pressure for 30 minutes
6. Release pressure naturally over 10 minutes

<u>Nutrition (Per Serving)</u>

- Calories: 213
- Fat: 2g
- Carbohydrates: 3g
- Protein: 3g

Subtle Mango Compote

Serving: 4

Prep Time: 10 minutes

Cook Time: 10 minutes

Ingredients

- 4 cups mango, peeled and cubed
- 1 cup orange juice
- 6 tablespoons palm sugar
- 3 tablespoons lime juice

How To

1. Add mango, orange juice, lime juice and sugar to your Instant Pot
2. Cook on LOW pressure for 10 minutes
3. Quick release pressure
4. Divide into bowls and serve
5. Enjoy!

Nutrition (Per Serving)

- Calories: 180
- Fat: 2g
- Carbohydrates: 12g
- Protein: 2g

Plum and Apple Medley

Serving: 4

Prep Time: 10 minutes

Cook Time: 15 minutes

Ingredients

- 1 plum, stoned removed and chopped
- 1 apple, cored and cubed
- 2 tablespoons avocado oil
- 2 tablespoons coconut sugar
- 1 cup apple juice
- ½ teaspoon cinnamon powder
- ¼ cup coconut, shredded

How To

1. Add plum, apple, oil, sugar, cinnamon, apple juice, coconut to your Pot and toss well
2. Close lid and cook on HIGH pressure for 15 minutes
3. Release pressure naturally over 10 minutes
4. Divide into bowls and serve
5. Enjoy!

Nutrition (Per Serving)

- Calories: 212
- Fat: 5g
- Carbohydrates: 11g
- Protein: 5g

Coconut and Avocado Pudding

Serving: 4

Prep Time: 10 minutes

Cook Time: 5 minutes

Ingredients

- 2 avocados, pitted, peeled and chopped
- 2 teaspoons vanilla extract
- 2 tablespoons coconut sugar
- 1 tablespoon lime juice
- 14 ounces coconut milk
- 1 and ½ cup water

How To

1. Take a bowl and add coconut milk, avocado, vanilla extract, sugar, lime juice and blend well
2. Pour the mix into a ramekin
3. Add water to your pot
4. Add a steamer basket and place the ramekin in the pot
5. Close lid and cook on HIGH pressure for 5 minutes
6. Release pressure naturally over 10 minutes
7. Serve cold and enjoy!

Nutrition (Per Serving)

- Calories: 190
- Fat: 3g
- Carbohydrates: 13g
- Protein: 4g

Rough and Tough (Yet Sweet) Lentils

Serving: 4

Prep Time: 10 minutes

Cook Time: 25 minutes

Ingredients

- 3 cups rooibos tea
- 1 tablespoon cinnamon powder
- 1 cup red lentils, soaked and drained
- 2 apples, cored, peeled and cubed
- 1 teaspoon cloves, ground
- 1 teaspoon turmeric powder
- Maple syrup

How To

1. Add lentils, tea, cinnamon, turmeric, apples to the pot and close lid
2. Cook on HIGH pressure for 25 minutes
3. Release pressure naturally over 10 minutes
4. Serve and enjoy with ample syrup on top

Nutrition (Per Serving)

- Calories: 200
- Fat: 4g
- Carbohydrates: 16g
- Protein: 7g

Crazy Pineapple Carrot Cake

Serving: 6

Prep Time: 3 hours

Cook Time: 35 minutes

Ingredients

- 1 cup pineapple, dried and chopped
- 2 carrots, chopped
- 1 and ½ cups whole wheat flour
- 1 cup dates, pitted and chopped
- ½ cup dry coconut flakes
- ½ teaspoon cinnamon powder
- 2 cups water

How To

1. Add carrots in food processor and pulse
2. Add flour, dates, coconut, pineapple and cinnamon to the processor and pulse
3. Add water to your pot
4. Add steamer basket and place a cake pan
5. Pour processor mixture in the pan
6. Cover and cook on HIGH pressure for 35 minutes
7. Release pressure naturally over 10 minutes
8. Keep in your fridge and slice
9. Enjoy!

Nutrition (Per Serving)

- Calories: 240
- Fat: 2g
- Carbohydrates: 11g
- Protein: 7g

10 minutes Lemon Cake

Serving: 4

Prep Time: 10 minutes

Cook Time: 10 minutes

Ingredients

- 1 teaspoon whole wheat flour
- ½ cup coconut sugar
- 16 ounces fat-free cream cheese
- ½ teaspoon vanilla extract
- ¼ cup coconut cream
- Zest of 1 lemon, grated
- 3 tablespoons lemon juice
- 3 eggs
- 1 and ½ cups water

How To

1. Take a bowl and add cream cheese, cream, sugar, flour, vanilla, zest, lemon juice and eggs
2. Whisk well and pour into big ramekins
3. Add water to your pot and add a steamer basket
4. Add ramekins and close lid
5. Cook on HIGH pressure for 10 minutes
6. Release pressure naturally over 10 minutes
7. Slice and serve

Nutrition (Per Serving)

- Calories: 212
- Fat: 5g
- Carbohydrates: 11g

- Protein: 5g

Apple and Pear Jam

Serving: 12

Prep Time: 10 minutes

Cook Time: 6 minutes

Ingredients

- 8 pears, cored and cubed
- 2 apples, peeled and cubed
- ¼ cup natural apple juice
- 1 teaspoon cinnamon powder

How To

1. Add pears, apples, cinnamon, apple juice to your pot and stir
2. Close lid and cook on HIGH pressure for 6 minutes
3. Quick release pressure
4. Use an immersion blender to blend
5. Serve and enjoy!

Nutrition (Per Serving)

- Calories: 212
- Fat: 5g
- Carbohydrates: 11g
- Protein: 5g

Chapter 11: Bonus: American Heart Association Lifestyle Recommendation

A healthy diet and lifestyle are perhaps the most potent weapon a man can wield against various forms of cardiovascular diseases and other health problems.

The simple steps outlined below are recommended lifestyle tips provided by the American Heart Association and are designed to ensure that you are keeping your body in tip-top shape!

Always try to use up as many calories as you have consumed.

This step is essential if you want to keep your weight in check and prevent from being overweight.

Always try to involve yourself in slight physical activity to keep your physical and cardiovascular health in check. Even you are unable to follow a regular strict routine, try to go for brief 10-minute sessions spread throughout your week.

The American Heart Association recommends at least 40 minutes of aerobic exercise of varying intensity (3-4 times) per week.

Try to eat from a wide variety of different food groups.

You may eat plenty of food daily, but that doesn't necessarily mean that you are getting all the required nutrients for your body.

Therefore, it is essential to mix things up and go for a nutrient-rich food diet that is packed with the right amount of minerals, protein, whole grains and other nutrients (but also low in calorie if possible).

This stable form of diet will help you to maintain your weight, blood pressure and cholesterol.

To summarize, try to emphasize on:

- A wide variety of veggies and fruits
- Whole grains
- Skinless poultry and non-fried fish
- Nuts and legumes
- Low-fat dairy products
- Non-tropical vegetable oil

Make your dietary choices around these recommendations

- Eat a variety of fresh and frozen fruits and vegetables (no high-calorie sauce or added salt/sugar)
- Try to choose fiber-rich whole grains for grain servings
- Go for poultry and fish without skin and prepare them in healthy ways (without adding saturated/trans fat)
- At the very least, try to eat 8 ounces of non-fried fish each week.
- Always try to opt for fat-free (skim) and low-fat (1%) dairy products
- Avoid foods that contain hydrogenated vegetable oils
- Limit the input of fat and trans-fat and replace them with monounsaturated, polyunsaturated fats.
- Try to cut back on foods and beverages with added sugar
- Choose food with less sodium and prepare meals with no added salt (detailed requirements are given in chapter 1)
- Try to minimize your alcohol consumption to 1-2 glass per day max

Make sure to quit smoking Tobacco and avoid second-hand smoke if possible!

This is pretty self –explanatory! Smoking not only hampers you and your health but also all the people around you, including your family members.

If you are already a frequent smoker, try to visit intervention groups or take nicotine patches to ease drawback effects.

Either way, it is best to leave the habit of smoking altogether or at least bring it down to a minimum.

Conclusion

I can't express how honored I am to think that you found my book interesting and informative enough to read it all through to the end.

I thank you again for purchasing this book and I hope that you had as much fun reading it as I had writing it.

I bid you farewell and encourage you to move forward with your amazing Low-Sodium journey!

38513679R00061

Made in the USA
Lexington, KY
09 May 2019